The Three Stages of Education.

AN ADDRESS

DELIVERED AT THE ANNIVERSARY

OF THE

COOPER FEMALE ACADEMY,

JULY 17, 1850,

BY SAMUEL W. FISHER.

DAYTON:
PRINTED AT THE DAILY DAYTON JOURNAL OFFICE.
1850.

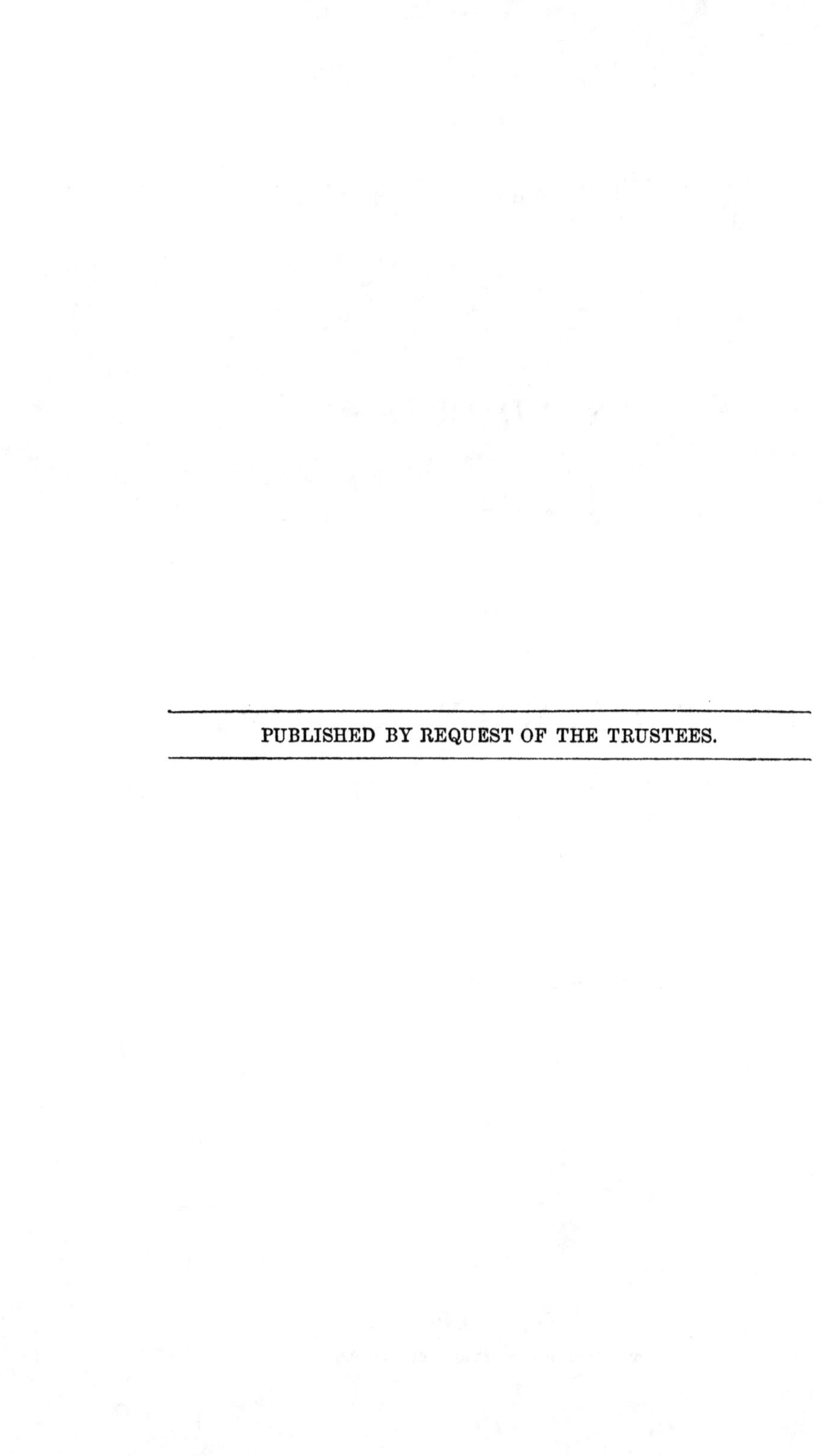

PUBLISHED BY REQUEST OF THE TRUSTEES.

ADDRESS.

It was the request of the Board of Trustees of this Seminary, that I should address you on this occasion, last year. For that engagement preparation had been made, when the providence of God prevented its fulfilment. A disease, whose advent and departure were alike robed in mystery, in its second journey around the globe, had reached our shores. Unheralded, it entered our towns and cities; its invisible breath prostrated thousands; its awful presence, felt rather than seen, or seen only in the terrible *results* of its power, spread the gloom of the grave-yard and the stillness of the Sabbath through our streets. The thronged marts of trade were solitary, the arm of industry was paralyzed, the hammer rang faintly on the anvil, the hum of untiring labor died away, the streams of life that rushed through our avenues, gave place to the solitary tread of the physician, the rattling of the hearse, and the slow moving procession of mourners. The teacher dismissed his scholars to their homes; the father gathered his family about him to wait together the issue; the pastor knew no rest while he ministered to the dying—performed the rites of sepulchre for the dead, and sought to comfort the living. In the midst of such a calamity, it neither became me to forsake my post for a day to fulfill my engagement in this city, nor was it possible for you to engage in the usual celebration of this anniversary. The address originally prepared for you, was subsequently delivered in another place and committed to the press. It would not be proper for me now to repeat that discussion or follow out substantially the same train of thought. But there was a division of the general subject on which I then was unable to dwell, that it is proposed to discuss on this occasion. In doing this,

I may have occasion to speak more of the *subjects* of Education than of the *theory*. In this there is one advantage. The theory of Education is old; it has often been developed by minds of the largest power in every age. But the *subjects* of Education are always new, fresh, rosy, joyous. *They* are always young. Generation succeeds generation, or rather, the wave of life behind melts into that before so imperceptibly that you cannot mark the point of passage; the new wave follows on, until ere it has dashed upon the shore, a hundred others have lifted their crests in pursuit. So childhood, ere it has grown to manhood or old age, beholds other childhoods, fresh and bright, chasing it onward. There is no stay, no growing old here. The laughing girl and careless boy are always in the foreground of life. Their merry voices, their light footsteps, their sunny brows are always new. Manhood looks back upon them with pride; old age grows young in their presence. They melt the frost from the heart; they unbind the cords of etiquette; they ungird the robe of artificial life; they bring us back to our original simplicity. Nature asserts through them her right in us. We wish we were boys and girls again; we would play ball in the same green; skate on the same pond; gather nuts on the same woods; rush from the old school house with the same wild, uproarious merriment; we would believe in quaint old Santa Claus again, and dream of his treasures, and hang our stockings before the widemouthed kitchen fire place in kindness to his yellow christmas coat; we would put our faith in Jack the giant killer, with his wondrous bean-pole, and seven-leagued boots and all the exhaustless treasures which our imaginations once discovered in the golden castles of our boyhood, if it were but for an hour. Refreshing it is to our hearts, disgusted with the artificial forms, and cold selfishness of society, to meet the blessed credulity of the child, and the vigorous hope of youth; to watch the young blood quicken in their veins and see the overflow of life, too soon to be confined within narrow conventionalities, and finally sink away into nerveless and trembling age.

Shakespeare divides life into seven ages. Of these, three belong to Education, considered with respect to this life.

These ages in which the young life prepares for its work, are designated by the nursery, the school, and society. Allowing from 24 to 30 years as the period within which most persons attain a fully developed character, from 8 to 10 years may be assigned to each one of these ages. The first has its chief influence from the nursery; the second from the school; the third from society. Let us visit first the nursery.

Babyhood and childhood, what are they but instinct and animal propensity? What have they to do with *intelligent* Education? Much, every way. They are wonderful *absorbents* of knowledge; they gain more intelligence than the other ages can bestow, and hold it much longer than that acquired subsequently. That infant, outwardly all animal, is a most diligent student. Smile upon it, and see its soul smiling in return; frown and lo! the eyes redden with tears. The babe is a student of physiognomy, and through that of the human spirit. Its mother's countenance is its first sun of science. Here all knowledge is centered. It entertains the profound idea of another spirit responsive to its own, months and even years before it can express such an idea in fitting language. Witness now its growth! It studies language. It masters the elements of articulate sound; it lisps the two simplest, dearest of words; instinctively it imitates human speech; the tongue grows lithe, the organs of voice are gradually trained to their work, till at length it has acquired the wonderful faculty of speech. In less than two years it has made larger advances in the acquisition of intelligent power, than the noblest brute ever did in all its life. It has begun, also, the study of physics, gymnastics, philosophy and morals. It begins to calculate distances; for the appreciation of distance is a matter of judgment. To the eye opened to sight from a congenital blindness, all things seem alike near. The child studies the qualities of things. The difference between a fall on a carpet or a stone reveals the soft and the hard. By sundry infallible experiments, it solves that great problem in philosophy, viz: that fire will burn; understands its qualities after the first burned finger, as well as Liebig himself, and never forgets them. It investigates the operation of the gasses, particularly hydrogen and oxygen when combined as water, and is as fully convinced of their power to produce suffocation, the first time the head is fairly dipped under, as Sir Humphrey Davy could be. Gravitation it investigates in various ways; but the great experiment which most effectually determines the question, is a tumble down stairs. Gymnastics very early claim attention. Legs and arms let off the superfluous activity months before the infant stands upright. What a proud day was that, parent, when your first born began to walk? to tread the earth no longer a feeble infant, but a self-sustaining, well balanced little humanity? How many trials in balancing! how many experiments preceded this feat, more magnificent than the most skillful exercises of the rope dancer!

At length this young walker and talker becomes a thinker. He questions every one; he pries into every thing. His "why?" "why?" shows that he is as intent upon studying causation as were ever Hume or Brown. He hears everything uttered; he ponders many a mystery that manhood cannot unfold. The whole of nature solicits his attention; his young intellect labors to get beneath the surface. Soon he experiments in various directions. He digs and plants, and then pulls up the germs to see *how* they grew. He turns mechanic, constructs, demolishes and rebuilds at pleasure. Again he studies engineering, momentum, and curves; and the best way to drive his arrow at the mark or his ball at his brother's back. He fashions his kite, sends it afloat, gaining a practical acquaintance with the resolution of forces, accomplishing a feat for him as great as that of Franklin, when by a similar contrivance, he brought the lightning from the clouds. Thus day by day, this restless spirit pushes itself out into the world of nature, gaining for the mind knowledge, for the hand skill, for the body vigor.

Meanwhile in the house another and higher style of Education is going on. He is beginning to understand the ideas of authority, of right, of truth, of generosity, of benevolence, of self-restraint, of manliness, of purity, of holiness, of God. For the outward and physical is only secondary; that which is moral and religious is primary. The first constitutes the form, the dress of life, mere external civilization; the second, the inward accomplishments of a soul with reference to eternity. Here then in these first ten years of his existence, a great part of the work in both departments must be effected. Moral influences mould the child day by day. As thought awakens, the passions kindle and the will grows strong, the parent watches, controls, indulges, limits, directs. Habit begins its lifelong reign. Impressions grave themselves upon the heart; prejudices possess the intellect; disposition unfolds, and the child takes the direction which manhood is to pursue. Between the child on the one hand, his parents, the family and the natural world on the other, there is at work, a silent, steady, unintermitted process of action and reaction. The inherent activity of the child, his exuberant energy, pushes him forward against everybody and everything. Mind, affections, body, are all intensely vigorous. You wonder how such unceasing activity can be found in so small a compass. You have heard of experiments in perpetual motion, but now you see it without an experiment, to your perfect satisfaction. You are astonished at the style in which the youngster will labor to effect a cherished purpose; the arguments, the promises, the tears brought to bear upon your opposite determination. The perverse activities of his growing spirit keep you ever on the look out. You seize hold of one and rein it in, when lo! another has pushed forth in a different direction. The guide of a child in this nursery age must be all eye, all ear, all hand, all thought, all love, all devotion and all patience. This is peculiarly the season of spontaneous activity. It is the luxury of new life and vigorous health. It is the age of knowledge acquired without application; of acquisition without conscious effort; when the external world is a novelty; when moral ideas are novel; when, like the forms in a kaleidoscope, the earth daily assumes some new shape of beauty to attract the young soul to itself. At this period the foundations are laid. In this spontaneous action, while as yet all is unformed in the expanding soul, the outlines of character are traced; the direction and general form is given, which can never be *wholly* changed; which can be partially modified only with great difficulty. It is within this period, the parent's *chief* work in Education should be performed.

Into this work two things enter. The one is direct guidance, instruction and restraint; the other the silent influences and attractions of personal character. The grape vine in Spring pushes forth its branches with great vigor in all directions. These for a time must receive support, direction and occasional pruning. Left to swing in the wind or twine themselves round whatever they may be near, is to expose them to ruin or greatly injure their productiveness. The place of every branch should be fixed long before it has grown into it. So the young spirit in the wild exuberance of its growth, demands the sustaining judgment and correcting hand of a parent. Its place should be fixed; whatever is evil controlled or removed, and right habits formed long before it attains maturity. For after it leaves the parent, it must pass into the hands of another husbandman, whose restraints and corrections may be severe and terrible. The young vine however must have more than guidance, support and restraint. The *sun* must shine upon it. In the shade, in darkness, it grows rapidly but feebly. Its joints are long; its body thin; its fruitbearing powers are almost wholly destroyed. The warm sun totally changes its character; condenses its juices, retards its outward growth; enlarges its fruitbuds, and invigorates it for the work of presenting to the vine dresser a luscious and abundant crop. Now the *silent* influences of parental character in the nnrsery are to young souls, what the rays of the sun are to the young vine. They rest upon them quietly; they act steadily and without interruption; they excite no opposition and can receive none; they insinuate themselves so like the light, into the heart of the young, that without understanding it the children are gradually moulded and affected thereby. Good principles, the seed of future power; good habits the form of future developements; good dispositions the elements of after fruitfulness; a secret force of self command and moral heroism, a strength of will for the right and powerlessness for the wrong; a love of truth and integrity of spirit; the recognition of authority and the habit of obedience to the infinite; all these, which in their ripeness constitute the noblest character, are formed and strengthened in the heart and mind mainly by the influences of parental teaching and *example*. The parents are the sun to the young heart. For a time they stand to it in the place of God. Through them Heaven pours its earliest and selectest influences upon the spirit. The beaming countenance, the tone of voice, the manner, the whole of a parent's life then affects it deeply. The mother is transparent to the child, long before the latter is to the former. The one is a great recipient; the other a great communicant. The one is to be fashioned and is therefore sensible to the least breath of influence; the other already fashioned is giving forth the plastic power. Thus if the parent be a true sun of pure and living light, the child will generally develope a character, which so far as human culture can effect it, will be prepared for the further work of education and of life. Such is the first age. The work of the nursery is the foundation of all the future, the most difficult and important, demanding the finest powers and issuing in the noblest results. No after training can fully correct a vicious nursery education. The form is given, that in the main is to last forever. A noble work this; worthy the noblest beings and the noblest powers, to preside over the formation of the character of a soul and make impressions that are not only to abide themselves, but which in long unfolding series are to produce fruits in others—fruits equally excellent and abiding.

Let us advance now to the second age of education—the *School*. The chief work of childhood has been accomplished; but however essential it is yet imperfect, however lasting it is only the foundation for the superstructure. As yet all the knowledge is elementary. The mind in its excursions has taken note only of external things; it has mastered that which is most necessary to its physical and moral well being, but it is far from that complete preparation which the business of life demands. It has gained a superficial acquaintance with external nature; but so has the savage. It has gained the elements of religious knowledge; but were it to remain in that condition, limited to those elements, it would remain a child forever. It has now to go beyond the surface and learn the secret composition and relations of natural objects. The idea of authority, obligation, obedience, has been wrought into the soul; it has now to learn what constitutes the true foundation of authority, what is the extent of obligation and the bounds of obedience due different authorities. Ignorant on these subjects the individual becomes the slave of prejudice; obeying where there is no just authority to command, disobeying where all the elements of authority exist. Ignorant of the physical world in its secret powers, he is unprepared to take advantage of and combine them so as to produce the highest form of civilization and enrich his outward condition. He has begun to look at the earth on which he dwells; he is now to study its extent, its structure, its divisions, its laws. He sees above him planets and stars moving in silent majesty; he is now to investigate their laws of motion and light, and ascertain the position which the earth occupies among these countless worlds. He has begun to know himself, his family; he must now enlarge his view spread his mind over states and nations, over the history of the past and the multiform aspects of the present. He has learnt the first principles of law, justice, integrity, benevolence; he must now proceed to ascertain their foundations and relations; to behold their operation in society; to discover the source of the evils that afflict the world, the experiments that have failed, and the fountains from whence the bloody streams of war have ever flowed; to understand the various institutions of civil society, the rise of nations in power, and, religion, the causes which, working secretly for long ages have most corrupted or most blessed mankind. He has begun to compass the elements of religious science, but now he is to enter upon the study of the higher truths of a spiritual world as they are found in the wide field of natural Theology—the all embracing providence of Jehovah—and the revelation made in his Word. To these truths, and others of a similar nature he is soon to address himself—these he must in part master or be prepared to master before he can take his place as an educated man.

In order to make these attainments, certain things are essential—1. The youth must gather together and pass in review the *facts*, in the just combination of which, all advanced science consists. These are to science as stones, brick and timber to a building. They are not science, any more than these, before being fitly put together, are an edifice; but they are the essential materials out of which, it is constructed. Without facts there is no knowledge, only fancies, theories, speculations, variable and fleeting as the clouds. The child who mistakes the forms in the sky for palaces and angels, is as just in his opinions as the man who takes the forms of his imagination for substantial realities. The neglect of facts, the disposition to create their appearances, and weave theories out of the brain alone, kept the world in darkness and held science back for centuries. The simple law of induction—letting facts reveal the law and not the law mould the facts—has given an amazing impulse to discovery, created new sciences, overturned fanciful pursuits and spread abroad among men the blessings of many admirable inventions. The disposition to theorize without facts—to generalize from a single fact or two; the indisposition to wait for the patient survey and analysis of a large number of particulars; the facility with which men can speculate, dream and build air castles, exists still. All around us are those who live in a region of theories unestablished; who dream in a world of realities, and at length die martyrs to their zeal in the cause of ignorance. Let the youth then learn patiently to gather up the sound materials of science; let his mind be ever awake to the forms and realities around him; let him search into the secret chambers of nature; let not appearances deceive him, but let him learn to wait until that which is substantial unfold itself, and he will be preparing himself for those rich possessions in science, which will alike ennoble the intellect, and fit it for usefulness.

2. In immediate connection with this gathering of the materials follows the training of the mind to use them for some

good purpose. The intellect must be accustomed to grasp, to combine, to separate, to classify. It must learn to reason on facts, to reach correct inferences, to make one result a firm foundation on which to proceed to a higher result. This power of arresting the processes of thought, of keeping the imagination in check, of discriminating between the false and the true, of holding the mind long intent upon a subject, and then having carefully examined its different aspects, arriving at just conclusions, is that which distinguishes the man of judgment and true science from the child and the charlatan. This power constitutes a possession most precious in all circumstances. It is an endowment that shines as lustrously in private life as it does in the marts of business, and adorns as truly the domestic circle as the forum and the pulpit. Destitute of this neither man nor woman is fully *Educated*.

3. In addition to these attainments, it is essential that the youth should master the language in which he is to communicate with his fellow men. He should investigate its copious vocabulary, its terms of science, its capacity for subtle thought,—for deep impression,—for the clear unfolding of his ideas on all subjects. This he should do in order to the acquirement on the one hand of a pure diction and on the other of a correct style of composition. The power of expressing himself in language clear, simple, correct and impressive, is of great importance. A lame, slovenly, ungrammatical style of speech, indicates the neglect of the noble instrument of thought and intercommunication between mind and mind; a failure to train aright that fine faculty of language, by which society is so much distinguished and blest. On the other hand the ability to write correctly, to commit readily and clearly his thoughts to paper, is of no secondary consequence. Essential in some pursuits, it is useful in all; nor can the youth justly regard himself as fully prepared for life, who has failed to attain the power of composition. These are three things which enter into the second style of Education. It is in making these attainments that the mind becomes disciplined for the after pursuits of time.

It is obvious that such acquisitions are not made either naturally, nor easily, nor in a brief period. They are the product of close application, continued for years and directed to subjects remote from popular view. They are such things as the young do not acquire spontaneously; such as most parents have neither the time nor the ability to impart. The youth has to go beyond things sensible; he must leave the outer for the inner world. This is always difficult. It requires application, direct effort, fixed times, abstraction from other objects, the instrumentality of books. Left to himself, after he has mastered that elementary knowledge which pours itself upon him at every step, he devotes himself to pleasure, to sensual gratification, to sports which however well they may be as recreation are ruinous when they constitute employment. Hence arises the *School* to meet this new stage of progress. Teachers, text books, and all the machinery of instruction come to the aid of the parent. The youth is isolated from the world, disciplined in classes, stimulated by a generous emulation, roused to put forth his latent powers by the foreseen position of influence and usefulness he can attain. Thus *habits* of study are formed; thus, one after another, difficulties vanish; the mind grows in science and power gradually but surely. The experienced teacher the admirable text book, the daily recitation, the private application, the freedom from other cares, the genial warmth of learning quickening the spirit, all combine to urge the youth forward in the training of his intellect. Thus the school fills up this second stage of education. Taking the child from the nursery, it forms his youth; it follows out the work of childhood and exalts him to a higher position in life, preparing him at length to test his principles and apply his intellect to practical affairs, when he goes forth into society. The school! Let me pause a moment over the sweet and bitter memories which cluster about that word. What visions of pothooks and trammels! of refractory, knotty, mispronounced and misspelled words! of verbs and nouns, and tenses and cases, the mysteries of grammar, rise before me! what a profound geographer was the lad who could repeat without failure the capital of every State in the Union! What an object of admiration the boy who could cypher in fractions and the rule of three? What a cyclopedia of knowledge was he who could tell the very day of the adoption of the Declaration of Independence, and could prove to our satisfaction that the sun did not rise in the east! How blessed was that season, when Webster's spelling book was a work of vast research, Dobell's arithmetic the sum of mathematical science, and our worshipful school master, next to George Washington, the greatest man in the Union! The joyous holidays—the trainings—the anniversaries—the vacations, how did the very thoughts of them once thrill the heart with pleasure; while alas! as if to vindicate the truthfulness of that old apothegm "there is no flower without its thorn," memory still retains the impression of sundry ferrulings and whippings administered, in the very spirit of Solomon's philosophy, upon our youthful persons, innocent of all evil but the eating of apples and trying the temper ot our pen-knives upon desks and benches!

Such was the School! Yet there the spirit of many a strong man was disciplined, for a noble future. Little by little we rose; gradually the prescribed course of instruction was gone over; one left for his farm, another for his trade, another for merchandise; the girls now ripened into young ladies passing off to keep them company,—while here and there, a solitary soul, destined by our fathers to other fields of labor departed for the sterner struggle of college life. The school! how vast its influence! how grand the results it has wrought out! how indispensable to the full education of the youn g The college may form the few, but the school is the mother of the many; the college may perfect the teachers, but the millions of the taught, who in time, as fathers and mothers are to teach the young in their first stage of education, who are to move the vast operaticns of human society, build cities and towns, reclaim the earth from its curse and bid it bring forth food and flowers, spread commerce from continent to continent and make the desert bloom with all the life of civilization,—these reverence the school as their "Alma Mater." From her walls they go forth possessed of the elements of intelligence and prepared to cultivate the bounteous heritage given to them of their heavenly father. They ascend the mountains—they fill the valleys—they cover the plains, they compass the sea, they sustain all noble institutions; and amidst all their wanderings they look back with thanksgiving to this their noble mother.

Let us pass now to the third stage of education—Society.—To some I may seem about to broach a novelty—a new term in Education. Imagining that the school or academy finishes *that* business, as full grown men and women they are abundantly qualified by previous discipline, to play their part successfully. It is true, indeed, that the foundation of character has by this time been laid and the edifice reared upon it. Yet it is equally true, that the structure has not attained all that completeness which fits it for the finest use. The walls have been reared and the roof thrown over, but the windows may be unhung, the doors without fastenings, the walls without plaster, the whole building without paint or ornament. In point of fact it is impossible in the second stage of Education, without prolonging it, to effect all these things. If we seek to erect only a log-cabin, with its appropriate furniture—a tolerable dwelling place—short time is necessary for the work; but if we wish to rear a structure that will combine stability, convenience, spaciousness and elegance, we shall be obliged to go through a far more elaborate process. In the school the intellect has been disciplined so as to enable it to advance; it learns *how* to think, without as yet having attained the chief results of thought; it is prepared to gain knowledge, it cannot go forth instinct with it. In this process of mental and moral discipline, some great principles are settled and a certain amount of knowledge material to success in life, attained. Yet in comparison to the whole field open to us, these results are very inconsiderable. The work of the school has been chiefly, to discipline the intellect, strengthen it to grapple with questions presented in after life, and afford it a sufficient acquaintance with general literature to enable it afterwards to prosecute the acquisition of it in any desired direction with ease and pleasure. When the girl leaves school, she has yet to go through another process of Education, before she can be fully prepared for the work of her life. As a young lady she enters her father's house and goes forth into society. What has she yet to acquire? She occupies, and is destined to occupy a two-fold relation—one to the *household*, the other to *society*. These relations are in reality closely connected, however much they may be generally separated. Her relation to the household is first in importance, and if rightly filled, she can with a true independence take her appropriate position in society. I am not derogating from the dignity of my theme therefore, in maintaining, as one thing indispensable to the well educated woman, the art of managing successfully the affairs of a household. By the ordinance of providence, in all civilized communities, this department of life falls to the female. It is not one to be slighted or despised; nor can it be mastered in a few days. It stands connected far more intimately than at first sight appears with the prosperity of the family, the happiness of individuals and the elevation of society. Many a man has been harassed and broken for life—lost to society and the world by a union with one who either through contempt of the attainment, or with the best dispositions, through early neglect, was unable wisely to conduct the affairs of a family. She who thinks the fingers that have touched the strings of the harp and the keys of the piano too delicate for housewifery; she who supposes that the genius instinct with poetry—the mind capable of dissecting Butler, and demonstrating Euclid, is of too refined a nature to descend to the study of the "Receipt" book and the management of a kitchen, had better renounce matrimony and betake herself to that fairy land where life is nourished without eating, and a genial climate permits nature to be satisfied with the slightest covering.

The first years of my life were passed in a large manufacturing town. Gentlemen from abroad occasionally sent their sons thither to undergo the training necessary to make them accomplished managers of similar establishments in other places. The young gentlemen, not unfrequently fresh from college, were obliged to commence their apprenticeship, by engaging in almost the lowest department of labor. From this they ascend through the different kinds of work until they had mastered the whole. In this way they became accomplished critics, understood precisely the character of the work produced, and knew how to direct others to do it. If there is any better way than this for you to gain a practical acquaintance with your appropriate duties as the guiding minds of a household, qualifying you either to direct others, or, if need be, perform the work yourselves, I leave for others wiser on this subject to determine. But be assured, whatever different opinions there may be about the best way of fitting yourselves for these duties, the subject is one that demands the most serious consideration—a part of your education in Socity which you may not neglect, without exposure to personal mortification, even should you be so happy as to avoid involving others in the consequences of your inexperience.—Could we trace out the causes which have given success in life to one, and witheld it from another of equal ability, I doubt not that the presence or absence of a faithful, wise, and diligent mind *at home*, would often be found among the most powerful. The world, in some of its features, may have changed since the time of Solomon; Society may wear a different dress and custom put on new forms; but the radical elements of private prosperity and happiness are unchangeable. The secret fountains are the same in every age. The streams may run in new channels, through new regions, amid new scenery; the plains and the mountains may spread and rise in new aspects, while the springs that feed the streams and fertilize the plains and gush from the mountain side, remain the same as the sources of blessing. So the costume of the virtuous woman whose price is above rubies, in the description of Solomon, may partake of the time and manners and customs among which she lived, but the ideas that are thus clothed in garments to us somewhat strange, express the essential qualities of a noble and useful woman in every age—of one who from the retiracy of her own home, sends forth an influence that crowns her children, her husband and her friends with honor. Happy will you be, if the world shall honor you through those whom your domestic virtues and home life have quickened and blest.

As you leave this place, however, there are still other relations you are to sustain, involving duties, imposing responsibilities and drawing after them results of no small importance. You now enter upon life in its more mature and earnest form. Parents, brothers and sisters, friends, claim you as co-workers in performing the duties devolving upon adult age. You take your position as young ladies in association with general society. The days of childhood and girlhood are past. As educated women, of disciplined minds, and formed judgments, you are called upon to bear your part in real life; to minister to the advancement of society, and share in all those practical efforts essential to its refinement and elevation. Immediately, on your entrance into these scenes, there commences a process of action and re-action between you and the new elements around you. Hitherto you have been the gay, careless spirit, a singing bird joyous in the mere consciousness of a vigorous existence, or you have been theorizing, speculating, looking at things in the abstract, disciplining the mind for future action. Now you enter upon the *practical* relations of life. Your opinions, if formed, are to be tested; if not fully formed, they are to be matured and settled amidst the conflicts of society. Principles are now to be applied to practice; the discipline of the mind made available in meeting questions which constantly arise. You are to converse so as to give and receive profit and pleasure. You are to shed around you a quiet, luminous, refreshing influence; not as noisy debaters, not as vociferous and random talkers, not as vain presumers on the license granted to youth and beauty, but as educated young ladies whose studies have invigorated their understandings and qualified them to act a sensible part in society. You will be obliged in your intercourse with others, to hear opinions that are crude and often false, sentiments not only untrue but of a most destructive tendency. Life and society are composed of heterogeneous elements. Various opinions and characters enter into their composition.—

It is in the friendly collision and intercourse of these, that God has ordained our faith, our general principles and courses of action, shall be firmly settled. Youth not unfrequently runs a most perilous course; the glory and the pleasure that lift themselves in the future, often blind it to the course of the current on which it floats, until the roar of the rapids suddenly falls upon the ear. Error is often urged by persuasive lips; mellifluous words, like honey gathered from certain flowers, may convey the deadliest poison, while truth may find utterance in plain, rude speech. Error may appear in all the fascinations of a winning sophistry, the principles of evil, robed as angels of light, may beckon us on into flowery paths, while truth and holiness may wear a homely garb and seem opposite to the joyous state of youth. There are two of Cole's pictures which at this time of your life, would form a most instructive study. I allude to "youth," and "manhood" in his voyage of life. The first, with its glory lifting itself so grandly in the future, while the current of life's river suddenly sweeps the voyager away from even the prospect of it; the second with its cataract and rapids below, and its scowling fiends and angel of mercy above, convey to the heart a lesson of actual life which, if you will but learn, will prepare you to meet many a temptation that, coming suddenly upon you, might prove too strong for the principles of good you now cherish. In this state of things, it belongs to your discipline for eternity, to learn how to discriminate the evil amidst its shows of beauty, the good, amidst its seeming evil. This is a high attainment in Education. It is one for which the nursery and the school may have prepared you, but which they cannot fully bestow. It is, in part, the work of society; it is to rise out of the intercourse with various and independent minds. Here in the collisions of sentiment and amidst the diversities of opinion, you are to justify this delightful description;

> "How charming is divine philosophy,
> Not harsh and crabbed as dull fools suppose,
> But musical as is Apollo's lute,
> And a perpetual feast of nectar'd sweets,
> Where no crude surfeit reigns."

The influence of society in moulding us, is more powerful

from being imperceptible. The young go forth into it, as if prepared to mould and fashion it after their own pattern. In the end it not unfrequently happens, that they are changed and greatly changed without being fully aware of the transformation. So a person in a skiff attempts to draw a frigate to himself; they approach rapidly, but it is soon manifest that while the latter may have moved an inch, the former has moved a mile. Society is already a formed, solid body, not easily affected by extraneous influences but rapidly influencing all who enter the circle of its power. While you give and receive influence, you will perceive the necessity of being on your guard against that overwhelming force which steals around and gradually moulds the young according to its own image.

There are three attainments, among others, which a young lady in this last stage of education should make. (1) A mature judgment. Of this you have laid the foundation in the school. But in society you have a wide field for its exercise, and numerous exigencies to develope it more perfectly.—There are some theories to discard, some imaginations to reduce, some day dreams to dissipate. The application of just principles to practice is a high attainment; it constitutes ripe judgment, it distinguishes one man above another for practical wisdom. The possession of such principles is a good thing, but it is a much better thing to be able to apply them just when and where they are most needed. There are some in whom correct principles are like loose jewels hidden and useless; there are others in whom they are like those jewels set by the hand of a master, and flashing forth their beauty before the eyes of men. There are some, who, with all their learning never learn how to act in society, so as to attain the confidence of others, and prosecute a successful plan of life; there are often others of far less intelligence who readily seize upon the true principles ot action and early learn how best to apply them, whose practical judgment and tact is worth far more, as an element of success and happiness, than the mere knowledge of books. Nothing tends so much to bring literature and science, in respect to female education, into disrepute, as the possession of these without the knowledge of life as it is, or the ability wisely to take advantage of circumstances and meet the oft recurring demands of society. It is one of the most important parts of education to attain the power of judging as by instinct of the true, the right, the pure, the appropriate, the profitable. The mind should possess a judgment like a flaming two edged sword, turning every way to prevent the entrance of evil into your own soul and oblige others to recognize its power.—This, however, is no gift of the schools. It must be gained fully in actual life, amidst the conflicting elements of society.

(2.) This judgment thus matured should then be sustained by firmness of purpose. Decision of character is not an appropriate attribute of a genuine *man* alone—it gives consistency and strength to the true woman. Guided by strong sense and intelligence, pervaded by gentleness and expressing itself in that refinement of manners which adorns her life, elevated far above obstinacy, it imparts stability to all that is lovely and precious, and furnishes a firm ground of confidence in respect to usefulness. A poet of the last generation writes

> Oh! woman in our hours of ease,
> Uncertain, coy, and hard to please,
> And variable as the shade,
> By the light quivering aspen made;
> When pain and anguish wring the brow
> A ministering angel thou."

Admirable as is the compliment in the closing lines, yet you will not regard it as redeeming the severe judgment of that which precedes. From that judgment you should seek to vindicate yourselves. No woman whose mind has been matured amidst the practical relations of society, and who has formed herself to decision in action, can properly be compared to "the shade by the light quivering aspen made."

(3.) Refinement of manners. True refinement has its source in the heart, and its deepest fountain is genuine religious faith. This you have been taught to seek as above all things most valuable. But the manifestation of those feelings, in any easy address that proclaims the desire to communicate happiness, is usually an acquisition of society itself. With manners refined and gentle, breathing the nobilty of kindness to all within your influence, without assumption or fear, without the boldness of the virago or the timidity of a bashful child; with this happy mean of gentleness, modesty and self assurance; ready to bear your part in the intercourse of life, and contribute your quota to promote the interests of society, you will have profited by the educational influence around you, and reached a position from which you may accomplish great good.

Thus these three things, mature judgment, decision and refinement in manners, are usually attained in their fullness only under the educational influence of society. In this connection, there are various and important topics on which the time allotted to this service will not allow us to dwell. One suggestion permit me to make, ere I close. If you would make these exercises of the school bring forth the richest fruits in society you must maintain the habit of study. It will be impossible for most of you to devote your chief attention to intellectual pursuits, as you have done here. Other and for the time, higher objects will claim your attention and exhaust most of your time and energy. But amid the most pressing domestic cares, there still remains in the lives of most women, ample room for a gradual but steady progress in the cultivation of the mind and the further acquisition of knowledge. The elevation you have here gained can be maintained only by the devotion of some portion of your time to the same studies which belong to the school.—The mind, although it can never wholly lose the quickening and elevating influence of your past course, may yet, through inaction or neglect, let slip many of its precious treasures, while its force of thought becomes weakened, and its intellectual resources receiving no enlargement, actually decrease as life advances. If you would fit yourselves to be indeed the noblest ornament and blessing of society, you must continue to commune with those intellects of the living and the dead, whose thoughts will enlarge the range of your vision, inform the understanding and purify the affections. Poetry, history, philosophy, theology and general literature, furnish some authors whose works in part, at least, you can master and find yourselves greatly gainers. Especially during the period that intervenes between the school and settlement in life, that halcyon period, when neither the strict regimen of the first, nor the oppressive cares of the second are upon you, when uncertain respecting the future, yet full of hope, buoyant with high animal spirits, and bright anticipations of a world you are just entering, you have leisure to accomplish much in this direction, with all the advantage of the freshness and impulse given to the pursuit, by the scenes from which you now pass. Then it is easy for you to confirm the habits here formed, and in doing that send your mind forward into higher regions of thought. An hour each day redeemed from sleep or pleasure, will in a few years accomplish wonderful results. It will not only make you respect yourself, but render you independent of those transient excitements so necessary to the enjoyment of others, by opening up to you sources of happiness far deeper, purer, and more abiding. If now you carry forward your education vigorously, for a few years in this direction, the acquisition of knowledge will be a habit and a joy, with which, should you be so circumstanced, the cares of a family will not greatly interfere. But if you wholly intermit these studies now, you will find it difficult to resume them in after life.

There are three courses which may be pursued on leaving the school. The young lady deeming herself fully educated according to the standard of those around her, delivered from the surveillance of teachers and ripe for scenes of pleasure, flings aside her books and devotes herself to present enjoyment. If she reads, it is only a work of fiction, or that which constitutes the froth of literature, something to minister a transient excitement, rather than nourish deep thought. If she plays, it is only to practice her old pieces for the evening's amusement. Dress, society, pleasure, form the cycle of her new life. There is no advance contemplated; neither life nor society is studied, nor the higher duties they impose understood and fulfilled. The judgment matures only by stern experiences. The immortal mind that might have gone on rising in knowledge and strengthening for life's great work, is satisfied with the pursuits of a butterfly, and content with the same kind of admiration elicited by that gay insect. Need I paint her future?

There is a second class, few in number, but rich in talents, in whom the love of literature and science has grown into the most absorbing passion; whose lives are consequently devoted almost exclusively to the interests of education, or the pursuit of knowledge. Here and there minds like those of Hannah Moore and Mary Lyon, appear in the past and present, so constituted originally and so improved by assiduous cultivation, and so animated by enthusiasm, as to be qualified to spread abroad a wide and deep influence, as among the best writers and educators of their age. Such minds now rare, as education shall more thoroughly discipline the females of the generations to come, will doubtless be multiplied; the fragrance and bloom of woman's spirit will enrich our literature, as well as bless the more limited circle of domestic life.

There is still another class. It embraces those, who, with a just sense of the high position of woman in society, seek to fill up the wide circle of her duties; who while they mingle in society, neglect not the fireside, while they minister to the enjoyments of home and the healthful intercourse of friends, yet seek the fountains of thought, which the wise and good of the past have opened; who, conscious of their imperfection, labor to extend the horizon of their experience and knowledge, while they bring the results of that labor to adorn the home they love, and ennoble their association with the world.

Such are the paths which open before you as you enter society. It will be for you now to choose whether the pathway of life shall conduct you through scenes of merely transient pleasure profitless for good, which will quell the ardent desire for advancement in the excitement of a present joy, and leave you at length, when the spirits of youth have departed and the bloom of beauty has vanished and the storms of life arise, like the inexperienced mariner, who, launched upon a sunny sea, neglects the favoring gales that would soon have wafted him beyond the reach of danger, and ere long beholds with terror, a darkened sky, the sea uplifting its angry surges and the port of hope yet far distant; or whether you will pursue that better path, in which, conscious of your nobility and the vantage ground for continued improvement, on which you now stand, you will nerve yourselves for a far greater work than you have here performed, you will resolve to make society itself impart to your spirit a richer grace and a higher degree of intelligence, you will form your minds to undertake the most difficult achievements, you will seek to gain by all the round of social duties and intellectual pursuits either incumbent upon or open to you, that more perfect, refined, and noble life of the soul, in virtue of which you will shine with increasing brilliancy, and shed around you a quickening power for good, even when age advances upon you; so that the charms of beauty, and the physical vigor of youth, as they depart will only reveal the concealed fruit now blushing into ripeness. Especially will this be the case, if what I have presupposed in all this discussion is true, and you have chosen that better part which cannot be taken from you. If to the accomplishments of literature and the graces and refinements of social life, you add that pure spirit of religion, which exalts whatever it penetrates, enriches poverty and pours the light of knowledge into the untutored mind of ignorance, assimilates man to God, and holds in blest harmony all the powers of the soul; which consecrates all our attainments to the noblest uses, opens ever fresh fields of action and usefulness, softens the ruggedness and relieves the painfulness of the darker hours of life, sheds a benison around affliction, and ministers a blessing through the sorrow of time; which will make you angels of mercy to our fallen race, and when you die, while the tears of loving and grateful multitudes your influence has made to feel the quickening power of a truly christian woman, shall be your noblest eulogy, the crown of life gemmed with stars shall be your unfading reward.*

Ladies and Gentlemen—There are no objects on which the eye of the stranger, as he enters our towns and villages, rests more gratefully, than on these public institutions. The private dwelling may speak of general prosperity, but it may be a purely physical prosperity, consistent, to some extent, with ignorance and vice. There may be, here and there, the evidences of an indomitable energy, and large individual accumulations of wealth, while the signs of the truest form of public prosperity may be absent. But when he sees broad avenues planned by no contracted mind, when he beholds numerous churches lifting their spires heavenward; when the temple of Nemesis rises before him in solid and majestic proportions, as if even the stern brow of Justice shall be wreathed in classic beauty; when institutions of learning, where the young are informed with intelligence, and their hearts moulded by wisdom, meet him at every turn, then a deep, calm joy enters his soul. He feels that religion, and law, and intelligence have here their home; that in these spacious mansions, and those more humble dwellings, taste and elegance and

---

*"What highest prize hath woman won
In science or in art?
What mightiest work, by woman done,
Boasts city, field or mart?
'She hath no Raphael!' Painting saith,
'No Newton!' Learning cries;
'Show us her steamships! her Macbeth!
Her thought-won victories?'

Wait boastful man! though worthy are
Thy deeds, when thou art true,
Things worthier still and holier far,
Our sister yet will do;
For this the worth of woman shows
On every peopled shore,
That still as man in wisdom grows
He honors her the more.

Oh not for wealth, or fame, or power
Hath man's weak angel striven,
But silent as the growing flower,
To make of earth a heaven—
And in her garden of the sun,
Heavens brightest rose shall bloom;
For woman's best is unbegun!
Her advent yet to come!"—Elliott.

purity dwell with enterprise and skill; that here must be the elements of a noble and an advancing society; that here are minds with whom his heart can sympathise and his spirit hold pleasant converse. Thus have I felt, as from yonder hill my eye first rested upon this beautiful city; thus have I felt still more deeply, as my intercourse has been increased with many of the intelligent, enterprising and the good among you; thus do I feel to day, on this most interesting occasion, on the anniversary of this cherished Institution—an institution devoted to the enlarged education of your daughters, where, under the most admirable influences, they may pass through the training of the school, and come forth prepared to take advantage of the perfecting discipline of society, and become, at length, not merely its ornaments, but plastic powers for the moulding aright of those who are to enter after them upon this moving scene of life. Happy is that people, whom religion, law, and intelligence ennoble. This trinity of influence will elevate them high in character, enrich them with the materials of power over men, and spread abroad the fame of their doings to distant lands. Under such influences, the spot where forty years ago the trees of the forest lifted their gigantic tops into the sky, now bears the beautiful city, rivaling those eastern Arcadias, which, for centuries, the hand of taste and wealth has been adorning. Let such influences mould our western world, and while Italy boasts of her artists, and her deep blue skies, and Greece rejoices in her Acropolis, and her land—one wide mausoleum of the immortal dead, and England exults in that learning, skill, and enterprise, which have given her dominion over the nations, *we* will rejoice in a nobler scene, in richer fruits, in a higher civilization, in a people pervaded with intelligence, exalted above poverty, obedient to law, yet bearing the impress of freedom, and living daily, not for the limited and selfish object of a merely personal prosperity, or a national aggrandisement, but in the spirit of the Immanuel to impart the light and hope of a better world, unto all the benighted dwellers on the earth, and raise the down trodden to a position in which they may possess the richest blessings of Time, and the fairest prospects for eternity.

www.ingramcontent.com/pod-product-compliance
Lightning Source LLC
LaVergne TN
LVHW011142110826
845150LV00008B/2468
* 9 7 8 1 4 1 8 1 9 3 0 3 4 *